HANDLEY PAGE
HERALD

TIMELINES

MATT FALCUS

First published 2015

Destinworld Publishing Ltd
3 Fairfax Road
Middleton St George
Darlington, Co. Durham DL2 1HF
www.destinworld.com

British Library Cataloguing in Publication Data.
A catalogue record for this book is available from the British Library.

ISBN 978 0 9930950 1 6

CONTENTS

ACKNOWLEDGEMENTS

A number of individuals have provided invaluable help in the research and production of this book. Of particular help at the photographers who have provided pictures from their collections. Each is credited with their pictures, but I would like to particularly thank Ron and Jim Smith, David Fraser, Ian Haskell, Chris Coates, Alberto Storti, Barry Friend, George Ditchfield and Leonardo Pin. I would also like to thank the late Harry Fraser-Mitchell of the Handley Page Association who proved an invaluable help in the early days of this project in providing material of great interest from the collection. I am only sorry that he was unable to see the finished book.

INTRODUCTION

The Handley Page Herald would ultimately struggle to make the impact on the Douglas DC-3 replacement market that the manufacturer hoped for. However, for a number of smaller airlines it was a perfectly suited aircraft for their needs. In this promotional picture two of those airlines show off their Heralds, with I-TIVE of Itavia Aerolinee and HB-AAG of Globe Air flying in formation.

In 1955, when the Handley Page Herald took to the skies for the first time, the world of commercial aviation was still dominated by the workhorses of the previous age. The Douglas DC-3 and its wartime C-47 variant had allowed many new airlines to begin services following World War II, and offered tremendous reliability and affordability, along with great availability due to the war surplus.

Airlines soon started looking to new technology to provide more comfort, prestige, and greater profits. Handley Page saw the opportunity, along with other aircraft manufacturers, to develop a replacement airliner for the DC-3 and other wartime piston aircraft. However, unlike other manufacturers, a like-for-like piston engine option was chosen whilst competitors such as Fokker looked to the turboprop in a bid to woo airlines.

Handley Page realised too late that the path they had chosen would not yield customers and backtracked to re-develop the Herald as a twin turboprop aircraft, but despite the quality of the finished product, orders would never be as significant as the Dutch rival's F-27.

The Herald nevertheless soldiered on with a variety of airlines worldwide until the 1990s, with a significant fondness from crews, passengers and those who had been involved in the aircraft's development.

As time passed, the few Heralds that remained in service in the late 1980s and 1990s enjoyed a renaissance as cargo carriers, ideally suited to the role with their robust construction and cheap operating costs. By 1998 the final operational aircraft flew its last flight and the type was relegated to the scrap heap and a few museums.

Photo © Barry Friend

USHERING IN THE NEW

The design of the Herald aircraft initially came about in the hope of attracting airlines who were operating wartime Douglas DC-3 aircraft and looking for a newer replacement. Seeking to fine tune its design, Handley Page consulted with many of these smaller airlines.

Handley Page Limited was founded in 1909 by Frederick Handley-Page. It was the first public company in the United Kingdom to start the design and manufacturing of aircraft. In its early days it was involved in producing bomber aircraft for use in World War I and II, including the highly regarded HP.57 Halifax which was used extensively in the latter campaign.

    The company was based at Berking until it moved to Cricklewood Aerodrome in 1912. When this airfield was closed in 1929, Handley Page moved its main headquarters to a new airfield at Radlett in Hertfordshire, although some construction still took place at Cricklewood until 1964.

In 1947 Handley Page purchased some of the assets of the Miles Aircraft Company, based at Woodley, near Reading, including many of the aircraft designs that had been produced prior to the company becoming bankrupts. One of these designs was for a four-engined airliner named Herald. The new company formed to look after the combined assets of Handley Page and Miles Aircraft was Handley Page (Reading) Ltd, and any aircraft designs produced at the Woodley site were designated with HPR prefixes. The prototype of the Herald was known as the HPR-3.

The Herald design emerged from an earlier airliner known as the Miles M.60 Marathon. This 20-seat all-metal passenger transport aircraft had four piston engines and had gained interest from both the Ministry of Supply and British European Airways, with orders for 25 examples each. Miles needed more orders to make the type justifiable, and soon became bankrupt. However, with the purchase of assets by Handley Page, production was revived under the new designation HPR.1 Marathon. Some 43 examples were built, although British European Airways

The four piston engined Miles M.60 Marathon became the H.P.R. 1 Marathon when Handley Page bought the assets of the bankrupt Miles Aircraft Limited in 1947 and started producing the aircraft. Ultimately the Herald design would emerge from the Marathon. Here two Marathons operated by Derby Airways, the predecessor of British Midland Airways, are seen. *(Photo Vic Seeley, via David Gauthier)*

When focus shifted to the Herald, Handley Page again favoured a high-wing aircraft utilising piston engines to carry passengers over a short range. It was anticipated that a great number of airlines operating Douglas DC-3 aircraft would soon require a more advanced, reliable and profitable airliner, especially since so many war-surplus 'Dakotas' had been press-ganged into service following the war to allow such airlines to form and build a business.

Seeking to fine tune its design, Handley Page consulted with many of the smaller airlines which were operating the DC-3 and other elderly aircraft. These airlines preferred to reduce the risk of upgrading their fleets by sticking with the tried and tested piston engine instead of the relatively new and expensive turboprop technology, which to date had only been seen on the Vickers Viscount airliner. The decision was made to equip the new airliner with four Alvis Leonides Major 14-cylinder, 870 horsepower, radial engines. This went against the original plan to use twin piston engines, but the required powerplant was not available with sufficient power.

Other specifications chosen for the HPR.3 as a result of consultations included capacity for 44 passengers, and the ability to convert the cabin to carry cargo with ease (including larger doors to make loading cargo easier). The cabin would be pressurised for passenger comfort and a cruising speed of 224 mph (360 km/h) would be achieved.

To make the aircraft more attractive to as many operators as possible, the Herald was designed to require a take-off run as short as 460m on unpaved strips, and yet still manage a range of 1,640 miles (2,640 km).

However, despite this positive start which, to Handley Page, seemed the correct solution to the needs of many airlines around the world as they sought new aircraft to upgrade their fleets, rival manufacturers were simultaneously working on solutions to the same problem and taking bigger steps to future-proof their designs.

DEVELOPMENT AND TESTING

Queensland Airlines was the first carrier to commit to the Herald from the drawing board. At this stage the aircraft was still in its four piston engine layout. Because of the order placed in 1954, the prototype aircraft G-AODE was unveiled to the public already wearing the colours of the Australian carrier and posed for various promotional photographs such as this one, around the 1955 Farnborough air show. Unfortunately Queensland Airlines retracted their order before the aircraft could be delivered, causing a major blow to the Herald programme. (Courtesy of BAE Systems Heritage Photo Collection, Warton)

The HPR.3 was officially named "Herald" in August 1954 and work on the prototype aircraft was advancing rapidly. Handley Page's sales team had already been drumming up interest from a number of airlines around the world, and had secured orders for 29 aircraft from Air Kruise, Australian National Airways, Queensland Airlines, and Lloyd Aéreo Colombiano. Based on the manufacturer's costs at the time, the break-even point was calculated at a rather low 75 aircraft, but Handley Page was confident of many more sales.

In the Netherlands, the aircraft manufacturer Fokker had started designing their own Douglas DC-3 replacement airliner in the early 1950s. Like the Herald, their F-27 "Friendship" was a high-wing aircraft capable of carrying 44 passengers, with the ability to operate from unprepared airfields and to convert its cabin to cargo configuration. However, unlike the Herald, Fokker had decided early in its development process to power their aircraft with the latest Rolls-Royce Dart turboprop engines. This option meant that only two engines were required to power the aircraft at cruising speeds of around 285 mph (460 km/h), with a similar range of 1,616 miles (2,600 km).

The first flight of the prototype aircraft took place from Radlett Airfield on 25th August 1955. However, the occasion was bittersweet as a variety of conditions soon led to the new aircraft no longer having any orders from the initial 29 received.

Air Kruise's, which was set to become the launch customer for the Herald, was taken over by British Aviation Services in 1953 and subsequently cancelled the order. Additionally, Lloyd Aéreo Colombiano had its contract cancelled due to financing issues. However, the major blow was when Australian National Airways and Queensland Airlines cancelled their orders in favour of the rival Fokker F-27, which was seen as a much better aircraft for their needs.

Handley Page continued to push their airliner, displaying it at the Farnborough Air Show in September 1955, still wearing the colours of Queensland Airlines. Yet airlines were not forthcoming in placing orders and, in the face of the imminent first flight of the turboprop F-27, the company was forced to rethink its strategy to salvage the aircraft they had spent significant time and money in bringing this far.

As a result of the emergency discussions, Handley Page announced that the Herald aircraft would be modified into a twin-engine turboprop airliner. Like its Dutch rival, it would be equipped with Rolls-Royce Dart 527 engines, each of which could provide over 1,900 horsepower. Other modifications included a 51 cm stretch of the fuselage and increased range. The new variant became the HPR.7.

Two HPR3 Herald prototypes were ordered in 1954 for construction at Woodley. They featured four 870 horsepower Alvin Leonides Major piston engines, with the first aircraft appearing in the blue, grey and white livery. Before completion, G-AODE was sent by road to Radlett before flight testing began. In the background, G-AODF is yet to be painted in the Handley Page house colours. (Courtesy of BAE Systems Heritage Photo Collection, Warton)

Prototype Herald G-AODE in Queensland Airways' livery departs from Farnborough following the 1955 SBAC air show.

The second prototype, G-AODF, first flew in August 1956. It is seen here at the Farnborough air show that year, attracting close inspection from airline executives no doubt considering which of the different aircraft one show could provide the future of their fleet needs. Note one particular person inspecting the interior of the Leonides engine.

G-AODF appeared at Farnborough again in 1957 and is seen here departing for a display to onlookers. Although Handley Page had been promoting the choice of four engines as adding safety, making the loss of one irrelevant to the operation of the aircraft, the same year would see G-AODE sent back to the factory for conversion with two Rolls-Royce Dart engines.

The Minister of Aviation discusses the Dart turboprops during an inspection of the re-engined Herald. The aircraft gained a British Certificate of Airworthiness to Transport Category (Passenger) to the highest standard following an extensive testing period, during which the aircraft operated impeccably.

The first three Herald series 100s were ordered in 1959 by the Ministry of Supply for British European Airways (BEA). All three aircraft, which would be registered G-APWB, C, and D, are seen on the production line at Radlett.

Workers prepare the fuselage walls and cabin floor during production of early Herald aircraft.

The high wing of the Herald matched the design of other emergent turboprops of the time, including the Fokker F-27 and Antonov An-24. It allowed easier access to the cabin for passengers and freight loaders who didn't need tall steps or ramps.

A crowded production line at Radlett with a significant batch of Dart Heralds in various stages of construction. The Hastings and Hermes line can be seen sharing the hangar in the background.

A batch of ten Heralds was ordered in 1959, starting with the initial three destined for BEA. Later, a batch of 25 was ordered in 1961. Modifications, such as the lengthening of the fuselage to 200 series standard, and the addition of a strengthened undercarriage to permit greater weight, would be incorporated on the line as production progressed.

A Herald airframe was used at Radlett for structural tests, measuring the effects of different pressurisations on the aircraft.

The pressure test airframe was gradually tested up to 4.5 psi – much greater than the maximum operating pressure of 3.35 psi which the aircraft had been designed for.

STIMULATING CUSTOMERS

DART *Herald* – Jet-prop airliner for everyone, everywhere

Once the Herald had been re-engined with Dart turboprops, Handley Page posed G-AODF for promotional photographs to advertise its new 'Jet prop airliner'. Initially the manufacturer continued to offer both piston and turboprop variants to customers, but soon focussed solely on the Dart engine model as airlines looked more increasingly to the better operating economics and technology of turboprops.

The modified HPR.7 Herald 100 series aircraft eventually flew for the first time on 11th March 1958, with certification being awarded the following month.

The modification had paid off, as an order was received from British European Airways for three HPR.7s to operate on its Scottish Highlands routes. By now Fokker had gained a huge advantage over Handley Page, with its F-27 having been in operation with customers for almost a year by the time the first production Herald flew on 30th October 1959.

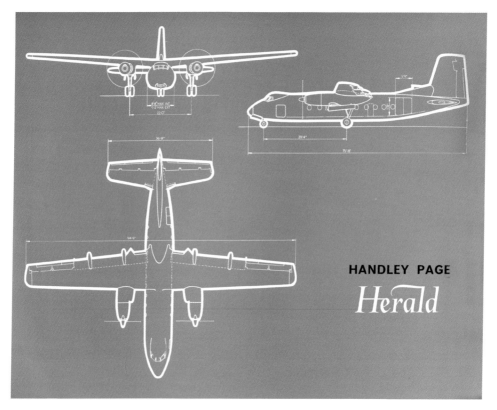

The dimensions of the Handley Page Dart Herald 100 series from three different angles, showing the redesigned turboprop variant of the airliner.

The impressive sight of HPR7 G-AODF performing a display at Farnborough Air Show in 1959. This aircraft was the second prototype and had previously appeared at Farnborough in 1956 and 1957 whilst still in the four-engine HPR3 configuration.

To further stimulate customers in its aircraft, Handley Page converted its second prototype aircraft into another variant of the HPR.7 – this time the 200 series. It incorporated a further 107cm stretch of the fuselage, increasing capacity to 56 passengers. The first flight of this variant was on 8th April 1961, following an order for six examples from Jersey Airlines.

Before Jersey Airlines took delivery of their own aircraft Handley Page leased G-APWA to the airline in 1961 to allow it to begin scheduled services with the type. The airline used the aircraft on flights from the Channel Islands to mainland United Kingdom. This shot sees 'WA still wearing basic Handley Page livery, and was taken shortly before the aircraft departed on its tour of South America with Prince Philip.

Commercial flights by the Herald finally began on 16th May 1961, ironically with Jersey Airlines using a leased 100 series aircraft. British European Airways began their Herald services in March 1962. Handley Page could finally show off their aircraft and sales, but they had a lot of ground to cover over Fokker's F-27, and a new rival in the form of Avro's 748 turboprop airliners which first flew on 24th May 1960. Despite the Herald's excellent performance, particularly on short runways, the F-27 was much roomier and the Avro 748 had better economics, leaving few airlines closing the deal on orders with Handley Page.

A number of sales tours had been conducted by Handley Page to airlines around the world, starting in April 1959. The tours took in India and the Near East, followed by South America, Australia and the Far East, and finally a tour of West Africa and South America in March 1960. During one demonstration, King Hussein of Jordan took control of the aircraft for over an hour as he evaluated the type for both civil airlines and his military operations, accompanied by Wing Commander 'Jock' Dalgleish of the Royal Jordanian Air Force, and Handley Page's chief pilot.

In November 1961 a tour took in Europe, the Near East and East Africa, attractive crowds of admirers as it demonstrated the aircraft to new customer Itavia in Italy. The following year a visit to Saudi Arabia demonstrated the type's excellent reliability and safety aspects.

However, one trip in particular stood out amongst all others when, in early 1962, the Queen's husband Prince Philip chose the Herald for his 11-country tour of South America. The choice of aircraft was important, with its excellent performance on short runways and unprepared airstrips vital for some of the destinations the prince would visit.

G-APWA was the aircraft of choice, provided by BEA, and fitted out with a special executive interior. Once delivered across the Atlantic, the aircraft began its tour in British Guiana, alongside stablemate G-APWC which had been flown out as a support aircraft for the trip. Countries visited included Argentina, Bolivia, Brazil, Chile, Colombia, Ecuador, Paraguay, Peru, Uruguay, and Venezuela. During the trip, 62 flight sectors were flown by G-APWA, of which Prince Philip personally flew 49 of them. The two aircraft on the trip flew 100,000 miles over 471 hours, including the outbound and return journeys to Britain.

Although not a sales or demonstration tour, the trip nevertheless placed a great deal of attention on the Herald due to its high profile passenger and pilot. Its reliability and serviceability record during the trip was excellent, and Prince Philip immediately sent a telegram to Sir Frederick Handley-Page upon his return to congratulate him on the Herald's "excellent service throughout my tour of South America".

Prince Philip at the controls of G-APWA during the 11 country tour of South America during 1962. His work on the tour saw him fly 99 hours and was intended to boost the significance of the type with potential airline operators.

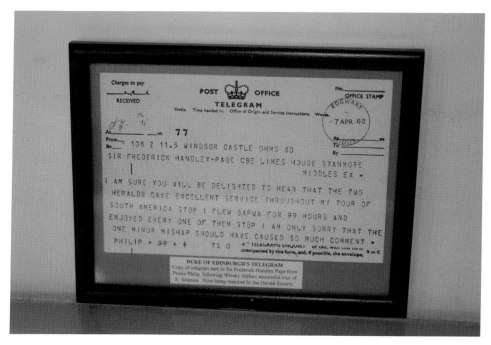

Following the sales tour of South America in Herald prototype G-APWA and G-APWC, during which Prince Philip flew 99 hours, he sent this telegram to Sir Frederick Handley-Page CBE to commend the 'excellent service' the aircraft gave. In the message he alludes to the 'minor mishap' which caused 'so much comment'. This refers to a fault in an electrical indicator, which was minor considering the two aircraft managed a combined 471 flying hours on the tour without any other incident.

The second prototype, G-AODF, approaches a grass runway during a test flight wearing the smart red and white Handley Page livery.

This promotional shot used as marketing material by Handley Page sees passengers leaving a Herald via the main door at the rear of the aircraft. Note that the aircraft has parked on grass.

On 24 May 1962, Herald G-APWC was called upon to leave its regular service operating Highlands and Islands services with British European Airways to carry royal passenger Princes Alexandra from London to Stockholm. She is seen here receiving flowers before boarding the aircraft. It would return five days later following her tour.

Two of the great aircraft produced by Handley Page fly in formation for this fantastic promotional shot. Alongside Herald prototype G-APWA is a Victor bomber, which was produced between 1952 and 1963 as part of the V-force.

Adding to the early bad luck of the bid to promote the Herald to customers was this crash of G-AODE on 30 August 1958. The day started with the aircraft departing Woodley and posing for photographs in formation with a Victor bomber over the Surrey countryside. It was then to fly on to Farnborough to take part in the SBAC air show. However, whilst cruising at 6,000ft part of the starboard Dart engine disintegrated, cutting a fuel line and causing a fire, before the engine separated from the wing. With the experienced Sqn Ldr Hazelden at the controls, the aircraft made a rapid descent – at times barely under control, and with the fire spreading to the tail plane – before undertaking a wheels-up crash landing in a field near Godalming. Amazingly all nine occupants walked away before the aircraft was overcome by the flames. Despite the incredible fortune that no-one was hurt, Handley Page would miss an important opportunity to demonstrate the aircraft to customers at Farnborough.

INSIDE THE HERALD

Keen to promote the possibility of turning the Herald into an executive transport aircraft, this example cabin layout shows how tables and dining furniture can easily be installed for the comfort of VIP users.

There were two production models of the Herald – the 100 and 200. The only immediate difference between the two was that the 200 offered a 107cm stretch, and thus greater capacity for passengers or cargo. The 100 series could seat between 38 and 44 passengers, whilst the 200 could seat up to 56, depending on the seat pitch used.

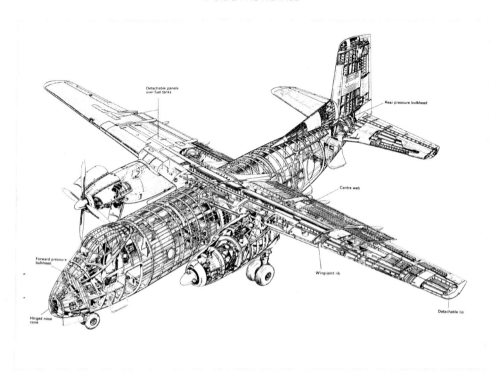

Technical Specifications:

Dimensions	Series 100 and 200
Wings Span	94 ft. 4.5 inches
Wing Area	886 sq. ft.
Root Chord	12 ft.
Tip Chord	6 ft. 3 inches
Aircraft Length	
(100 series)	71 ft. 11 inches
(200 series)	75 ft. 5 inches
Tail Span	36 ft. 9.5 inchest

Engine Specifications:

Two Rolls-Royce Dart Series RDa 7/2 Mark 527 turboprop engines of 1,910 s.h.p. plus 505-lb jet thrust.

The four Alvis Leonides Major 14-cylinder, 870 horsepower, radial engines originally installed on the Herald were later replaced by two Rolls-Royce Dart 527 engines, each of which could provide over 1,900 horsepower.

The passenger cabin featured large, round windows, and a large double door on the rear port side of the aircraft allowed both passengers and cargo to be loaded with ease. Given the fact that the cabin floor was less than a metre above the ground, the Herald boasted the ability to be able to load without the need for full-sized airstairs, or in fact any stairs that it could not carry itself.

In the cockpit, the Herald accommodated a crew of two pilots, with dual controls and instruments in each position. It was designed to be comfortable, and made easy for pilots to reach their seats without the need to crouch or squeeze past equipment.

A slightly unusual style of passenger seating is demonstrated here, along with the overhead rack, window curtains and modern (for the time) décor. Cleanliness, space and colour would hopefully attract airlines looking to upgrade from the basic comforts of the ageing Douglas DC-3.

A promotional image showing the standard scene inside the Herald, with two seats either side of an aisle which is wide enough for a full cabin service. Above, an open baggage rack provides enough space to store small items.

An example of a Herald passenger cabin with forward and rearward seating set around a table.

The galley space at the front of the cabin, alongside the cockpit entrance and main passenger door. It was capable of heating food and drinks for the passengers accommodated on board.

The cockpit of the prototype Herald, G-APWA, now preserved at the Museum of Berkshire Aviation at Woodley. Pilots considered the Herald very comfortable to fly and, although basic, its cockpit was clear and fit for purpose. The yellow weather radar can be seen on the right of the picture.

The standard cabin layout for most Herald aircraft in passenger service saw a 2+2 layout of seating for around 50 passengers. Behind the seating area a door gives access to the freight hold alongside a toilet.

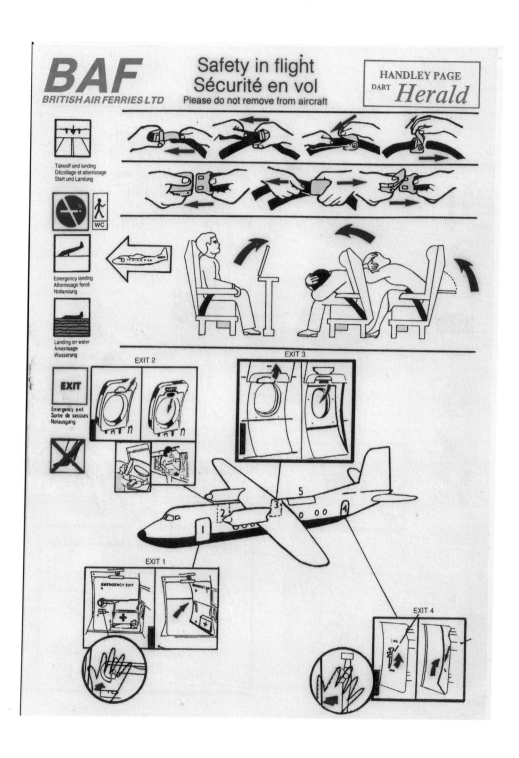

The seat-back safety card from a British Air Ferried Herald demonstrating to passengers the safety features and procedures in the event of an emergency. Looking closely, you can see some of the unusual locations of emergency hatches, such as in the roof of the cabin.

AIRLINES AND OPERATORS

One of the final passenger operators of the Herald, Air UK flew 11 of the type until 1984. (Photo © Ron Smith)

In total only 50 Herald aircraft had been built when production ceased in 1968, despite the sales and demonstration tours around the world, and the aircraft's excellent flying records during this time. To put this in perspective, the Fokker F-27 went on to sell 586 airframes between 1955 and 1987, whilst the Avro (later Hawker Siddeley) 748 sold 380 airframes. Of the Heralds built, the following airlines and operators owned or leased aircraft.

Aerosucre Colombia

Two Heralds were taken on by this Colombian airline in 1981 to fly internal passenger and cargo flights. One of the aircraft crashed on 5 November 1989.

Aerovias

The Guatemalan airline Aerovias took two Herald aircraft, one in 1987 and one in 1988. The aircraft operated passenger and charter flights. They operated until the late 1990s.

Air Anglia

Two Heralds were acquired by Air Anglia in 1975, operating scheduled passenger services from its Norwich base and other UK destinations both domestically and, in particular, to Amsterdam Schiphol in the Netherlands.

Air Ecosse

Air Ecosse leased Heralds occasionally from British Air Ferries to transport oil workers to Aberdeen from 1978.

Officials from Handley Page and Air Manila exchange a model of a Herald aircraft to commemorate signing an order for two aircraft in 1965.

Air Manila

This Philippines airline ordered two Heralds in 1965, with deliveries taking place the following year. The type introduced reliable inter-island services to many remoter destinations, owing to the type's ability to operate into rough-and-ready strips. The airline temporarily ceased operations in December 1969 and, when the government decreed that Philippines Airlines was to be the only national airline in 1973, Air Manila was forced to shut down completely. However, limited charter flights were resumed in 1974 with one Herald until its eventual retirement in 1979.

Three Air UK Heralds and a Fokker F27 share a busy ramp at Southampton Airport in 1984 (Photo © Barry Friend)

Air UK

The newly formed carrier had a fleet of 11 Heralds, alongside Fokker F-27s and F-28s. It was a Herald that became the first aircraft to wear the new airline's striking blue livery. The aircraft would eventually make way for the F-27s by 1984 as the airline looked to future modernisation.

ALIA Royal Jordanian Airlines

The Jordanian national airline received two Heralds from the Royal Jordanian Air Force in 1963 to help it establish domestic and tourist routes. One of the aircraft was lost in a crash in April 1965, and the type was replaced by jet equipment in 1965.

(Photo © George Ditchfield)

Aligiulia

A small Italian regional airline which leased two Herald 200s between 1985 and 1986 for domestic flights. Unfortunately the carrier soon collapsed and both aircraft were briefly stored before finding new roles with Channel Express.

Arkia Israel Airlines

Two Heralds were ordered in 1963 by Arkia, an airline flying domestic routes within Israel. It later added three more examples. The type flew alongside the airline's Vickers Viscounts and became a common sight in Israel on the many internal routes. The aircraft remained with the airline until it received modern replacements in 1977.

(Photo courtesy of AJJ Collection)

Autair International

In 1963 Autair International leased three Heralds for use on its European holiday routes. The type proved popular with passengers, and aircraft utilisation was high during the summer period. By the end of the year the aircraft were returned, and Autair's crews were sent to train pilots of Alia and the Royal Jordanian Air Force on the type. In 1966 BEA disposed of its three Herald 100s, selling them to Autair International for use on its growing domestic network.

When Autair was renamed Court Line Aviation Ltd in 1970, the Heralds were sold on to Lineas Aereas La Urraca of Colombia.

Bahamas Airways

A single Eastern Provincial Herald was leased to Bahamasair for four months in 1964 and used on inter-island and Florida routes.

Bavaria Fluggessellschaft

Three Heralds were acquired by the Munich-based independent airline for use on cargo and passenger charter routes from 1964. Their aircraft were also sub-chartered to Arkia Israel Airlines from 1967. All three aircraft were sold back to Handley Page by 1970.

(Photo © Peter F Peyer)

British Air Ferries

BAF purchased three Heralds from Eastern Provincial Airways in January 1975, flying from its Southend base. The following year a further four Heralds were sourced from Arkia and TransBrasil respectively. In 1977 it became the world's largest operator of Heralds when all eight examples of the Royal Malaysian Air Force were acquired and gradually brought back to the UK in a mixture of liveries. The airline operated its examples mostly in a configuration that allowed both cargo and passengers to be carried.

Many of BAF's Heralds were operated on behalf of, or registered to, different organisations flying cargo, newspapers, tourists, and supporting the oil and gas industries. One was even leased to SATA Air Azores briefly in 1978. A further seven Heralds were leased from British Island Airways.

British European Airways (BEA)

Once Handley Page had redesigned its Herald aircraft as a twin-engine turboprop, the Ministry of Supply ordered three examples for use by British European Airways' Scottish 'Highlands and Islands' services. These series 100 aircraft entered service in January 1962 (however, two aircraft were initially leased to Jersey Airlines).

The Heralds allowed BEA to continue serving the remote airports in Scotland which in most cases had short and under-prepared runways, for which the aircraft was ideally suited. The type replaced the DC-3 aircraft previously used on the routes, and route proving flights operated in 1961 caused a stir to many residents of the remote communities of Islay, Campbeltown, Grimsetter, and Kirkwall, who had never seen turboprop aircraft fly into their airports. After four years, however, many of the airports had improved their infrastructure and BEA introduced its larger Vickers Viscount aircraft on the majority of services, with the Heralds taking up a supporting role.

BEA sold its Herald aircraft by the end of 1966, ending a short association with the type. Nevertheless, the order for these three examples enabled Handley Page to set up their production line and begin building Heralds for customers.

(Photo © Jim Smith)

British Island Airways

Formed upon the separation of BUIA from BUA in July 1970, British Island Airways maintained the eight Heralds and refined its route network to focus on profitable services from the Channel Islands and other UK airports to destinations around Europe. It later added another three aircraft, and also operated cargo charters to take advantage of the Herald's mixed capabilities.

Despite adding jet aircraft to its fleet, BIA still felts its Heralds necessary for a number of roles. It added a new livery in 1977, and continued to grow with the acquisition of Air Anglia. In 1979 the carriers were merged to form Air UK.

(Photo courtesy of AJJ Collection)

(Photo © Ron Smith)

British Midland Airways

Two Herald series 200s were ordered in 1964 by Derby Airways, shortly before it was renamed British Midland Airways. It saw potential in operating the type on services to the Channel Islands, and also in carrying freight. After the aircraft left the fleet in favour of the Viscount, three more Heralds were acquired in 1973, being incorporated into the airline's extensive domestic network. The Heralds were withdrawn in 1977.

G-APWF at Southend in 1968 (Photo © Barry Friend)

(Photo © Ron Smith)

British United Airways (BUA) / British United Island Airways (BUIA)

By 1963 Jersey Airlines had been merged into the Channel Islands subsidiary of British United Airways. Its Heralds were eventually repainted into the colours of BUA, and it even took a seventh example for use in a VIP configuration. Others were later sourced from different airlines, growing the fleet which was at times deployed to a number of different bases.

In 1968 the Channel Islands division, along with Manx Airlines and Morton Air Services, were devolved of BUA, and became British United Island Airways (BUIA).

Brymon Airways

Brymon Airways acquired one of British Midland Airways' Heralds, G-ATIG, in 1977 and used it to fly between Newquay and London Heathrow. It later flew on other domestic routes, but was sold in 1982 to Janus Airways.

Euroair Transport

A British regional operator, Euroair Transport operated a number of types including the Embraer 110, Vickers Viscount, and HS.748. It also leased a couple of Handley Page Heralds in 1986.

Europe Aero Service

When Globe Air ceased operations, France's Europe Aero Service (EAS) took delivery of its former Herald fleet (comprising two aircraft) in 1968. It used these from its base in Perpignan, and also from Paris, on European and domestic routes. They were also used on charter work, and were seen in a variety of the airline's colour schemes before being sold on in 1988.

(Photo © Leonardo Pin)

Far Eastern Air Transport

Two Heralds were ordered by this Taiwanese airline in 1965, becoming the first British aircraft to be operated on the island from their delivery in 1966. Other second-hand examples were also sourced, used (as the manufacturer intended) to replace older Douglas DC-3 aircraft. Sadly one example crashed in February 1969, killing 36 people.

The deal is done. Globe Air executives sign for an order of two Heralds in 1962.

Globe Air

This independent airline from Switzerland ordered two Herald aircraft in 1962, with deliveries in 1963; they also decided to take an additional two aircraft. They were flown primarily on holiday charter routes around Europe and North Africa, achieving a high utilisation and reliability. Sadly the airline ceased operations in October 1965 following a loss of public confidence after one of its Britannia aircraft crashed.

Guernsey Airlines

A small independent airline offering scheduled services to the Channel Island of Guernsey. Formed in 1977, it leased Herald G-ASVO from British Air Ferries in 1983 to bolster its capacity.

Gulf Air

Bahrain's national airline leased a couple of Heralds from British Air Ferries briefly in 1977.

(Photo © Alberto Storti)

Itavia

Officially known as Aerolinee Itavia, this independent Italian airline ordered two Heralds in 1961, replacing Douglas DC-3 and de Havilland Heron aircraft. A third example was also acquired, and the type flew on charter flights to southern Europe, and Italian domestic schedules. The airline ceased operations in February 1965.

Janes Aviation

A British cargo charter airline, Janes Aviation leased a Herald from Nordic Oil Services in 1990.

(Photo © David Fraser)

Janus Airways

Not to be confused with Janes Aviation, Janus was an air charter carrier based at Coventry and Lydd airports in the UK. It was owned by Hards Travel, which organised holiday tours to Europe. In addition to two Vickers Viscounts, the airline acquired Herald G-ATIG from Brymon in 1982. It also used G-BAVX, G-BDFE and G-BEBB briefly. The carrier ceased flying in 1985.

(Photo courtesy of AJJ Collection)

Jersey Airlines

The first commercial orders for the Herald came from Jersey Airlines as the SBAC air show at Farnborough in September 1960, following the twin-engine redesign. The airline was impressed by the 'high potential' of the Herald over short-range routes and airports with short runways, on which it would employ the type. This came after evaluation of all turboprop aircraft on the market at the time, and was a major boost for Handley Page.

Despite ordering six series 200 aircraft, Jersey Airlines initially leased two series 100s that were destined for BEA. On the airline's five daily return flights between Jersey and London Gatwick, the Herald was able to carry 500 passengers, compared with 320 on the Douglas DC-3 aircraft that had been used prior to its arrival.

Lineas Aereas La Urraca

A Colombian scheduled airline, Lineas Aereas La Urraca purchased three Heralds in 1970 that had previously been used by Autair. The aircraft were used on flights from Villavicencio. All three aircraft ended their days with the airline, with two being involved in serious accidents.

(Photo courtesy of AJJ Collection)

Maritime Central Airways / Eastern Provincial Airways

Maritime Central Airways of Montreal, Canada, purchased two Heralds for its Nordair subsidiary in 1961, with deliveries taking place the following year. These were used on services to remoter destinations in the north of the country.

When Maritime Central separated from Nordair in March 1962, it ordered two of its own Heralds. Then, in 1963 it purchased Nordair outright, including its Heralds and route network. Maritime Central itself was purchased by Eastern Provincial Airways the same year. It cancelled the order for two Heralds, as it had two examples of its own, taking the total in the fleet to four examples. The aircraft were ideal for the remote and unprepared airstrips used on some of the airline's routes.

One of the aircraft crashed in March 1965. The other three were sold on to British Air Ferries in 1975 after many reliable years serving remote regions of Canada.

MMM Aero Service

A small domestic airline carrying cargo and passengers within Zaire. It was formed in 1981 and took two former British Air Ferries Heralds. One of the pair, 9Q-CAH, crashed on 10th September 1984 killing 30 people following an engine failure, resulting in the airline closing down shortly afterwards.

Nile Valley Aviation

An Egyptian company which undertook aerial photographic survey work, Nile Valley would lease Herald aircraft from British Air Ferries for a few months at a time from 1977. They would also be used on tourist charter flights whilst on loan to the airline.

(Photo © Christian Volpati)

Shortly after returning from service with Sadia, third prototype G-APWA sits at Southend Airport awaiting its next duties. It would go on to fly for a number of cargo carriers before being preserved at Woodley.

Sadia / TransBrasil

Sadia became the first customer for the Herald in South America when it pursued an order in 1962. However, owing to difficulties with the Brazilian government in obtaining permission to acquire the foreign aircraft type, it was not until 1965 that an order was made. Two aircraft were leased to the airline by Handley Page in 1964 to allow evaluations to take place, which served to strengthen its belief in the type, and also once again prove its ability to replace the Douglas DC-3. Six examples were in operation by 1968.

Sadia was renamed TransBrasil Lenhas Aereas. It sold three Heralds in 1973, and the remaining three were sold in 1976. However, their sale was not before three examples were sent to operate to remote airfields in northern Brazil by an airline known as TABA in an attempt by the government to improve air transportation links within the country. Despite its initial reluctance to allow the Herald to operate in Brazil, this final move was testament to how revered the type became because of its operational performance.

(Photo courtesy of Chris Coates)

SEA South East Airlines

A very short-lived airline which operated Heralds on lease during 1987 on short haul routes from the United Kingdom.

Styria Airlines

Operating a daily route from Graz in Austria to Klagenfurt, Innsbruck and Frankfurt, Styria Airlines used their single Herald, leased from Itavia Airlines, during 1970.

Trans Azur Aviation

TAA was an airline formed as a joint venture between British Air Ferries and St. Tropez Airfield in May 1981 in the hope of developing passenger services from the region. Herald G-BCWE was transferred from BAF to the new airline and registered F-BVFP, wearing a hybrid colour scheme. However, the airline was not a success and ceased operations in October 1983.

MILITARY HERALDS

A postcard image showing a Herald operating for the Royal Malaysian Air Force, with personnel milling around the aircraft. Closer inspection reveals that this aircraft is G-APWA, the Herald prototype. It was leased to the RMAF at the end of 1963.

The Herald 400 series was a specifically designed military variant built as a freighter version, but ultimately identical to the 200 series. It included a side cargo door, and was set up to carry extra weight, carry stretchers, or act as a parachute platform.

It is understood that the Royal Air Force had intentions of ordering the military Herald variant, which it favoured over other designs of the day. However, Sir Frederick Handley Page had taken exception to the British Government's desire to merge his company with another manufacturer as part of rationalisation plans. As a result, Handley Page was denied an order, which went instead to the Hawker Siddeley Andover. Over 30 aircraft were ordered, which operated between 1966 and the early 2000s.

The two military operators of Herald aircraft were:

King Hussein of Jordan took control of a demonstration Herald aircraft during a sales tour as he evaluated the type for both civil airlines and his military operations His air force subsequently took delivery of the type, with two later being transferred to the new national airline, Alia.

Royal Jordanian Air Force

Following the sales demonstration tour in 1960, King Hussein ordered three examples and became a qualified pilot on the type. All three were actually 200 series aircraft, but allowed the operation throughout the Middle East and into difficult airfields with troops and cargo. The three aircraft were transferred to national airline ALIA in 1963.

A Royal Malaysian Air Force Herald, FM1024. This aircraft later flew for British Air Ferries, and was written off when it crashed into a mountain in Colombia whilst flying for Aerosucre.

This Herald 401 was delivered to the Royal Malaysian Air Force in December 1964 as FM1026. It was sold to British Air Ferries after 13 years of service. Seen here shortly after returning to the UK and now registered G-BEYJ, its former identity is clearly identified by the blue and white livery still worn.

A RMAF Herald in service.

Royal Malaysian Air Force

When the Royal Malaysian Air Force was formed in 1958, it soon looked for a transport aircraft that could operate to all corners of the country. It ordered eight Handley Page Heralds, with the first delivery in November 1963. The air force effectively ran a scheduled operation from its Kuala Lumpur base, and occasionally a Herald was converted into VIP configuration.

The aircraft were used extensively but not intensively. They underwent numerous upgrades and repairs, and were involved in supply drops, airlifts, and the dropping of propaganda leaflets.

The RMAF Herald fleet was sold off in 1976, with the aircraft going on to civil operators elsewhere in the world. Given the low amount of hours that had been flown in air force service, there was still plenty of life and value left in them.

A daring demonstration of the versatility of the Herald as G-ARTC, wearing the colours of Maritime Central Airways, acts as a platform for parachutists. This was one of the selling points for the newly formed Malaysian Air Force.

CARGO RENAISSANCE

Channel Express Herald G-SCTT arrives at Bournemouth Hurn on a cargo flight. Channel Express became one of the biggest operators of the Herald, and also became the final airline to operate the type. (Photo © Ron Smith)

The final operators of Herald aircraft were cargo airlines. Channel Express became the largest of these, emerging out of Express Air Services in 1983. It would have the prestige of operating the final Herald flights in 1999.

In its twilight years, many smaller operators found the capacity and operating economics of the Herald perfect for short freight work, such as mail and courier services. Elan was one such operator, flying nightly out of East Midlands Airport. British Air Ferries would also make use of its Heralds for freighter work.

BAC Charter / BAC Express

BAC Express was a cargo charter airline which leased Heralds from Channel Express when required.

Channel Express would be the final operator of the Herald, retiring its last example in 1999. It primarily operated the aircraft on flights for the Royal Mail. Two examples are seen here at Glasgow awaiting their next flights. (photo Ron Smith)

Channel Express

Following the formation of Jersey European Airlines, the operations of Express Air Services were rebranded as Channel Express in 1983. The Herald aircraft continued to operate mail flights. A number of Heralds were sourced from a variety of operators, and the airline became the last to operate the type when it was finally retired in 1999.

This Herald was leased from British Air Ferries and painted it in the colours of Elan Air, the forerunner to DHL. It operated nightly freight charters from airports such as East Midlands.

Elan

Elan Air was formed in 1982 to operate cargo and package flights on behalf of DHL. Its base was East Midlands Airport in the UK. The airline would be rebranded as DHL Air, but not before the Heralds had been disposed of.

Express Air Freight

Two former Arkia Heralds joined Express Air Freight in 1977 to fly cargo routes from the mainland UK to Jersey in the Channel Islands. Later two more Arkia aircraft were acquired, and the airline expanded into night time mail flight, and passenger charters. It later merged with Intra Airways, and would become Jersey European Airways in November 1979.

Janes Aviation

A British cargo charter airline, Janes Aviation leased a Herald from Nordic Oil Services in 1990.

Panavia Air Cargo

Operated Heralds in Central America during the 1980s, including G-APWA and G-BAVX. The tail featured a stylised 'PAC' logo.

Securicor Air (later Securicor Express) operated this Herald for three years between 1983-86.

Securicor Air

Amongst the most brightly coloured Heralds seen was G-AYMG when it operated for Securicor Air – a freight company based at Birmingham Airport. It was later rebranded as Securicor Express, but eventually the aircraft was sold to Channel Express in 1989 after six years with the airline.

Westair International

A Herald was leased by Westair International for cargo flights in the UK between 1988-89.

HERALDS TODAY

The most significant Herald preserved today is the third prototype, G-APWA, which is at the Museum of Berkshire Aviation on the former site of Woodley Airfield. It is preserved in the colours of British European Airways (BEA).

The final operator of Herald aircraft was Channel Express in the United Kingdom.

A number of Heralds can still be seen preserved or withdrawn from use. The most significant of these is the first production HRP.7 series 100 aircraft, G-APWA. This is the first aircraft to commenced Herald passenger flights when it was leased to Jersey Airlines in 1961, before joining BEA, Autair, the Royal Malaysian Air Force, Sadia, Transbrasil, and TABA. Its final operator was British Air Ferries, however, also significant is that this aircraft performed the royal tour of South America with Prince Philip at the controls for many of the flights.

G-APWA is today preserved in the colours of BEA at the Museum of Berkshire Aviation, on the site of the former Woodley Airfield near Reading. Today the airfield is gone, but the small museum seeks to preserve the history of the site, and presents this complete Herald aircraft for visitors to enjoy. On-board are displays of the type's history, and it is possible to experience the cabin and cockpit as travellers and pilots would have.

Air UK was a major operator of the Herald during the 1980s. Two of its former aircraft are now preserved in the United Kingdom for the public to visit. The first, G-APWJ, is at the excellent Duxford Aerodrome, which is home to the Imperial War Museum and a variety of civil aircraft.

The second Air UK example is G-ASKK, which started life with Autair International and also flew for British Midland, British United, and Sadia. It is now on display at the City of Norwich Aviation Museum at Norwich Airport – an airfield from which Heralds were a common sight for many years. Alongside it is a preserved Fokker F-27 also in Air UK colours, allowing the visitor to compare first-hand the two rivals from the fight to develop a successor to the ubiquitous DC-3.

At the Yorkshire Air Museum, near York, one of the last Heralds to fly is on display. G-AVPN retired in the late 1990s after flying as a freighter for Channel Express Air Services for a number of years. However, this aircraft began life with Bavaria Fluggesellschaft before joining Itavia, British Island Airways, Air UK, and Nordic Oil Services. Unfortunately in recent years this complete airframe has been reduced to only the cockpit section, with the remainder being scrapped. Its ultimate future is unknown.

For a number of years a preserved Herald stood proud on top of the observation deck at London Gatwick Airport's South Terminal. A former Arkia Israel machine, it later flew for Channel Express and was a popular attraction for visitors to Gatwick. However, following the closure of the observation deck the aircraft has been languishing in a forgotten corner of the airfield and its days are surely numbered.

For visitors to Scotland, the cockpit of Herald G-ASVO, yet another Channel Express aircraft which had become damaged after colliding with a light pole at Bournemouth Airport in April 1997. Today it is on display at the Highland Aviation Museum at Inverness.

The cockpit section of G-BEYF, another former Channel Express Herald, still exists. It has recently been moved to the Bournemouth Aviation Museum after spending time in storage at Wycombe Air Park.

(Photo © Ian Haskell)

TIMELINE

The significant events in the timeline of the Handley Page Herald.

Date	Event
19th May 1946	Miles Marathon makes maiden flight at Woodley.
Late 1952	Handley Page design team set task of designing a Douglas DC-3 replacement.
1953	Larger Marathon, dubbed HPR3, proposed by Handley Page.
25th August 1955	First HPR3 Herald prototype, G-AODE, makes maiden flight. Re-designated HPR5.
September 1955	First public appearance at SBAC display, Farnborough.
24th November 1955	First flight of the Fokker F-27 competitor.
20th July 1956	HPR5 Certificate of Airworthiness awarded.
3rd August 1956	Second prototype flies.
June 1957	Conversion to twin-engine turboprop begins.
11th March 1958	Modified HPR7 makes first flight from Woodley with Dart 527 turboprops.
August 1958	HPR7 Certificate of Airworthiness awarded.
30th August 1958	Prototype G-AODE crashes on publicity flight. All aboard survive.
17th December 1958	Second HPR7 prototype flies.
10th April 1959	Demonstration tours begin. 44 countries visited in 26 weeks.
June 1959	BEA orders three Herald 100 series for 'Highlands and Islands' services.
December 1959	King Hussein of Jordan takes control of Herald G-APWA on demonstration flight.

March 1960	Demonstration tour to West Africa and South America.
1st February 1961	Two Heralds ordered jointly by Maritime Central Airways and Nordair.
8th April 1961	Prototype modified into 200 series, with stretched fuselage.
June 1961	First delivery to Jersey Airlines.
September 1961	Itavia orders two Heralds.
November 1961	Demonstration tour to Southern Europe and East Africa.
5th January 1962	First Herald delivered to BEA.
11th January 1962	11-country Royal tour of South America with Prince Philip at the controls for many flights.
13th February 1962	Nordair begins Herald operations.
November 1962	Globe Air order four Heralds.
1962	Demonstration tour to Saudi Arabia.
1962	A Herald is used to set the record for the highest free-fall when paratroopers jump from 34,350ft.
12th April 1963	Itavia begins Herald operations.
4th May 1963	Globe Air begins Herald operations.
November 1963	Arkia orders two Heralds.
8th November 1963	Royal Malaysian Air Force (RMAF) begins Herald operations.
December 1963	Alia Royal Jordanian Airlines begins Herald operations.
January 1964	SADIA begins Herald operations.
1st May 1964	Bavaria Flug-Gesellschaft begins Herald operations.
9th September 1964	Derby Airways (later British Midland Airways) orders two Herald 200s.
10th April 1965	Alia Herald JY-ACQ crashes at Demas, killing 45.
June 1965	Far Eastern Air Transport orders two Heralds.
16th February 1966	Far Eastern Air Transport begins Herald operations.
18th March 1966	Air Manila begins Herald operations.
3rd November 1967	Sadia Herald PP-SDJ crashes near Curitiba, killing 21.

18th July 1968	Europe Aero Service begins Herald operations.
15th August 1968	Last Herald built is delivered to Arkia as 4X-AHN.
24th February 1969	Far Eastern Air Transport Herald B-2009 crashes at Cheluchien, killing 36.
October 1970	Lineas Aereas La Urraca begins Herald operations.
2nd November 1972	La Urraca Herald HK-718 crashes, killing 12.
January 1975	British Air Ferries (BAF) purchase first three Heralds.
2nd March 1975	Air Anglia begins Herald operations.
10th January 1977	Brymon Airways begins Herald operations.
19th November 1980	First herald flies in Air UK colours.
1987	Final passenger flight of a Herald, operated by British Air Ferries.
1998	G-BEYF of Channel Express operates the final commercial flight of a Herald.
1999	G-BEYF retired. Final Herald flight.

PRODUCTION LIST

Construction Number	Series	Last Registration	Other Registrations	Status
147	100	G-AODE		Crashed UK, 30/8/58
148	100/ 200	G-ARTC	G-AODF	Scrapped
149	100	G-APWA	PP-ASV, PP-SDM	Preserved Museum of Berkshire Aviation, UK
150	101	HK-718	G-APWB	Crashed Colombia, 2/11/78
151	101	HK-715	G-APWC	Scrapped
152	101	HK-721	G-APWD	Crashed Colombia 7/5/72
153	201	G-APWE		Scrapped
154	201	G-APWF		Nose preserved Jersey, UK
155	201	G-APWG		Scrapped
156	201	G-APWH		Remains on fire dump, Norwich, UK
157	201	B-2009	G-APWI	Crashed Taiwan, 24/2/69
158	201	G-APWJ		Preserved Duxford, UK
159	201	9Q-CAH	CF-NAC, G-BCZG	Crashed Zaire, 10/9/84
160	211	CF-NAF		Crashed Canada, 17/3/65
161	211	G-ASKK	PP-ASU	Preserved City of Norwich Aviation Museum, UK
162	210	B-2001	HB-AAG, G-ATHB	Derelict Taiwan

163	204	PI-C869	G-ABSP	Scrapped
164	203	G-ASBG	I-TIVA	Scrapped
165	207	B-2011	109, JY-ACR, G-ATHE, D-BOBO	Scrapped
166	206	TG-ASA	C-FEPI, G-BCWE	Scrapped
167	206	9Q-CAA	CF-EPC, VP-BCG, G-BDFE	Scrapped
168	203	I-TIVE		Crashed Italy, 4/11/70
169	207	JY-ACQ	110	Crashed Syria, 10/4/65
170	210	G-AVEZ	HB-AAH, PP-ASW	Scrapped
171	401	G-BEYD	FM1020	Scrapped
172	401	G-BEYE	FM1021	Scrapped
173	S210	G-SCTT	G-ASPJ, HB-AAK, F-OCLY, F-BLOY	Scrapped
174	209	G-BEZB	4X AHS	Scrapped
175	S401	G-BEYF	FM1022	Cockpit preserved Bournemouth Aviation Museum, UK
176	213	G-AVPN	D-BIBI, I-TIVB	Cockpit preserved Yorkshire Air Museum, UK
177	214	G-ATIG	PP-SDI	Scrapped
178	401	HK-2701	FM1023, G-BEYG, HK-2701X	Crashed Colombia 16/9/91
179	213	G-AYMG	D-BEBE	Scrapped
180	401	HK-2702	FM1024, G-BEYH, HK-2702X	Crashed Colombia 5/11/89
181	401	G-BEYI	FM1025	Crashed Malaysia, 17/1/76

182	401	TG-ALE	FM1026, G-BEYJ	Scrapped
183	209	G-BAZJ	4X-AHR	Remains on fire dump, Guernsey, UK
184	203	G-BBXI	I-TIVU	Scrapped
185	214	G-ASVO	PP-SDG	Forward fuselage preserved Highland Aviation Museum, UK
186	S214	G-CEAS	PP-SDH, G-BEBB	Scrapped
187	401	G-BEYK	FM1027	Scrapped
188	S210	G-STVN	HB-AAL, F-OCLZ, F-BOIZ	Scrapped
189	209	G-OTAG	G-ATDS, 4X-AHT	Scrapped
190	214	PP-SDJ		Crashed Brazil, 3/11/67
191	214	TG-AZE	PP-SDL, G-BDZV, F-BVFP	Scrapped
192	215	RP-C866	PI-C866	Scrapped
193				Test fuselage; scrapped
194	214	G-DGLD	PP-SDN, G-BAVX	Scrapped
195	209	G-CEXP	4X-AHO, G-BFRJ, I-ZERC	Stored London Gatwick, UK
196	203	G-BBXJ	I-TIVI	Remains on fire dump, Jersey, UK
197	S209	G-GNSY	4X-AHN, G-BFRK, I-ZERD	Scrapped